Confessions of a
BEADAHOLIQUE

Stone
CRAZY

Crystal M. Stephens

To order additional copies of this book, contact:
Xlibris
844-714-8691
www.Xlibris.com
Orders@Xlibris.com

ISBN: Softcover   978-1-4568-0185-4
        Hardcover   978-1-4568-0186-1
        EBook   978-1-6641-3403-4

Library of Congress Control Number: 2010915780

Print information available on the last page

Rev. date: 09/28/2020

DEDICATIONS

To God be the Glory, He helped me tell my story
About me and BEADS, then B.E.A.D.S. in me
Which created this book full of Beadalousity

To my Mother Joyce and Father the late Nathan W. Stephens
Thank you for teaching your children to be the best at whatever we choose to do.

To my sisters Rachelle and Marsha and my brothers Nathan, Wendell and Mark
My son Christopher, grandsons Cameron and Carmelo, my Robert, Tasha, Lena, Lil Bit, Kia, Bria
and Ernest Jr.

To my Pastor and Overseer Bishop Maureen L. Davis
Open Door Mission True Light Church, Philadelphia, PA
Your messages are the Truth and so Encouraging!

To The Honorable President of the United States of America
Mr. Barack H. Obama
Thank You for allowing me to dream through you
A dream that has now come true

To the Federal Court Judge, who judged me?
By the content of my character

Thank you to my brother Wendell
Your words of encouragement have been a driving force.
I did it Kevs! Our family has another Author. Now it's your turn.

To my Friends Cornelius and Sharon
Thank you for listening to
Crystal, RieRie, Beadella, Beadsz and
plain old crazy me, through good times and bad

To my bdsf Ern: It's gonna be nice!

To my Family - I Love You All

To my brother Mark
To my nephews Johnathan and Julian
Thank you all for your attempts to place my bead world
on canvas, no matter how crazy it seemed

To Everyone who has allowed me to bead my love into your lives.

INTRODUCTION

Hello! My name is Crystal. I am a Beadaholique (bead-a-hol-ic). So…you've never heard this word? Humm. Well, you may not find it in a dictionary or a thesaurus. Spell check certainly saw red every time I typed the word; yet this word is real. It's time the world became aware that beaders, beadiacs, beadaholiques, etc. exist. Beadmania has arrived! Along with this warning: Beware, Beadaholiqueism may be contagious.

The jewelry, home and fashion industry of today consistently confirm my opinion that anything can be beaded. Beads that bling are on so many things! When I go shopping I see them on displays, shelves, mannequins, racks and walls. Clothing, hats and shoes bling. Curtains, sheets and bedspreads bling. Beads bling on furniture and appliances. Beads bling on things that I've seen in my dreams. If I had my way I would drive a car detailed with beaded bling and bumper stickers saying: "Beadaholique on Board"-"Will stop to shop for beads"-"Honk! If U bead too!" Are you getting a visual? LOL.

You are about to enter my bead world. It contains real stories, pictures, poems, songs, and drama. God's gift of creativity is truly amazing. What has come to life through the craft of beading has driven me to take on this book challenge.

If your having what I call a (bbd) bad bead day, turn it into a (gbd) good bead day, take a moment to B.E.A.D. The day will certainly turn out to be a God blessed day full of Love, Laughter and Creations.

A BEADAHOLIQUE IS:

- ONE WHO LOVES AND LIVES TO BEAD

- ONE WHO IS EXCESSIVELY FOND OF BEADS

- ONE WHO MAKES BEAD TRANSFORMATIONS

- ONE WHO RECALLS CRAFT EVENTS

- ONE WHO WRITES POETRY ABOUT BEADS

- ONE WHO MASS COLLECTS BEAD MEDIA

- ONE WHO RESPONDS TO THEIR CREATIVE PASSION

- ONE WHO WRITES SONGS ABOUT BEADS

- ONE WHO SHARES A PASSION FOR BEADS

- ONE WHO SEES BEADS IN A NEW LIGHT

TABLE OF CONTENTS

CONFESSION

ONE WHO LOVES AND LIVES BEADS

Have you ever heard the saying "confession is good for the soul?" Well it is! When you confess it is not only good for the soul but for the mind and body too! A true confession is like a spring cleaning or a fall organizing of the mind . A confession creates a clear path that is ready to complete a mission. My mission is to tell the world about my passion for beading. I want to share my excitement about the craft by allowing beaders and non beaders to see beads as I see them. You are about to venture into my bead world. During the course of this book, I plan to take you on a passion packed journey, because I believe if you are passionate about something you can take it to infinity and beyond!

I love to make things bling. My definition of bling is taking something that is plain and transforming it into a colorful 'beadeliciously' beautiful object. This is accomplished in various ways. For instance, if I take an article of clothing like a tee-shirt and add paint, glitter, sequins, stones or just a lot of beads, it will bling. It transforms from plain to elaborate. Any article of clothing can be beaded. Beads on other things are works of art; also known as bead art. Bead Artists make sculptures out of beads in the form of animals, dolls, toys and etc. There are even beaded pictures. Have you noticed that the world is full of beads? A stone covered, bead blinging, crystal rocking revolution has begun. Beads are not used just for jewelry anymore. They are used in the oddest places you can imagine. Like the city I live in, there are walls filled with beaded bling. We have beaded gardens and beaded ponds. The use of natural stones makes these places stonemazing yet manmade beads are used too. When you take the time to recognize and appreciate stones/beads; beadaholiqueism (bead-a-holic-kism) awareness begins. So many beads, so little time to make things with them. If you make your own beads, so little time to create beads, then make creations out of them. The possibilities are endless which allows new creations to be endless. As you read further you will see a method to my bead madness, opps! I meant: gladness.

My family and friends when they call me on the phone or text me, often ask me (right after saying hi); What are you doing? Are you playing with those beads? Are you in Beadland? You love those beads don't you? So I respond by saying: yes! But don't worry I'm with friends. Listen. I have a good time playing with my beads. They are user friendly. They even talk to me, not audibly but in their own special way they holler "string me". I'm never bored, I have my beads. I've even been called "beadbrain". Well hello! Beadbrain is writing a bead book. How do you like me now?

When I told my brother Wendell (aka Kevs) that I was writing this book and gave him the title, he immediately responded by asking: Do you have an oath or creed? (most holics do). Kevs is an Officer in one of our nation's armed forces. It was the perfect question. By the way, all three of my brother's are career servicemen. It took very little time to come up with an oath for Beaders. I call it: The Beader's Creed. This Creed is dedicated to those who bead all around the world.

Each chapter is dedicated to a definition of Beadaholique. I hope you are ready for a bead adventure. Every time I thought of something else to say about beads, I felt like I was going on an amusement park ride. The ride begins then suddenly comes to an end and you have to get off. When you really enjoy the ride, you do not mind getting back in line so you can experience the thrill again. So let's start the ride! You are now approaching the end of chapter one so climb aboard…

YOUR BEAD ADVENTURE IS ABOUT TO BEGIN

STONE CRAZY

* ONE WHO IS EXCESSIVELY FOND OF BEADS*

One day after shopping for beads at one of my favorite craft stores, I met my beaddopted sister/ friend (bdsf) Ern at her mother's house. While sitting on the sofa, I began to show her my most recent bead purchases. We were oohing and aahing so much that her mother Eunice wanted to know what all the excitement was about. After we answered her, she responded by saying to us; "You all are **Stone Crazy**!" Well! We started laughing so hard we had tears in our eyes. I am also known for creating a song on demand so I got up from that sofa and started singing. Before I knew it, I had created a bead song. The words and the music entered my head as if the song already existed. Laughing while singing only produced more tears. We had taken a ride on a bead-a-go-round which gave me my book title along with the song to accompany it: "You're Stone Crazy Girl". She was right. I am Stone Crazy! Keep reading! You might agree with her.

I want to tell you how I get my shop on for beads. This type of shopping is adventurous too. You see there are so many different ways to do it, all resulting in great satisfaction. Let us explore a few ways to bead shop.

My first choice for bead shopping would be a local craft store. In some of these stores, the section containing beading materials and supplies have many long aisles. These aisles are categorized by bead types. I invite those who have never been within a bead aisle to take a trip to a craft store to explore one. The bead types are also divided into sections according to the manufacturer. Once you get an eye full of all the beads, move on to the bead medians and tools. There are various ways to get those beads strung and stringing leads to blinging. String/thread is the most popular bead median. Some other bead medians are elastic, leather, wire, rope, chain, lace, etc. My favorite is nylon-coated wire. It comes in many sizes and colors. These colors are what make the aisles so inviting. A few times I became so mesmerized, rainbows filled my eyes. I could see and sing a rainbow. You know the rainbow song : "red and yellow and pink and green, purple and orange and blue. O.K. O.K., where was I? I will confess that I have been called "Rainbow Bright" too. A very colorful compliment I might add. Colors like words are very powerful. I surround myself with color, in clothing, home décor, and jewelry. The beads in my life are also very colorful. Which allow my creations to burst and bling. If you are going to take the challenge to buy, let me, suggest that you select one or two colors to work with your first time around. Beading starter kits are available too, with everything needed to make a finished project if you want to take the easy route to beaded bliss.

The Natural Stone aisle is where you will find the precious and semi precious stones. Other aisles contain glass, crystal, metals, gold, silver, plastics and more. It may also be a good idea if you are bead shopping for the first time, to explore one aisle per visit until you become more familiar. Be sure to get a store circular to find out what's on sale. Bead shopping can be costly; especially if you like to shop. When I first got a touch of what I call bead bug, it was fatal. My personal cure was to own every bead in the store. I spent over my budget on several visits. I was so excited about beads I shopped and shopped for them. You know a definition of bead is: anything that has a hole in it and can be strung. Well there you have it, two holes in my head and totally strung OUT! Eventually I had to set aside bead-shopping money. I was buying them just because they were colorful and pretty. Before I realized what was going on, I was the proud owner of thousands of beads. Then I had to shop for storage containers, wall units, label makers, etc. to organize and store them. It took hours to sort, label, and store them. Now I select a focal bead (center of attraction) then travel up and down the aisles to select the rest of the beads to finish my design. This is a cost effective way to bead shop. It has saved me money and space that unused beads occupied. I still occasionally buy a few odd beads but now I can complete my designs at one sitting because I have the beads I need. Having variety is good but try not to let things get out of hand.

My next choice for bead shopping would be a supplier's catalog. Most of them are shipped free of charge. When you can't get to a store, a store comes to you. Looking through a bead catalog is like reading a good novel. It gets better and better as you turn each page and you never want it to end. Beading supply catalogs are thick and full of color too. Then after placing an order you wait anxiously for the arrival of your package. I have compared the packages that arrive at my door to presents. Knowing what's inside does not even matter.

Shopping on-line is another great way to shop for bead stuff. These websites are beadeliously colorful, mesmerizing and without a doubt: full of beaded goodies. I thought the few hours I spend in stores was something. Well let me tell you, shopping on the world wide web (www) can become timeless. You get to shop all around the world wherever a bead for sale exists. Websites have no opening or closing times so if a 6:00 am shopping crave hits, it can be satisfied. There are individuals who make one of a kind, special beads with websites. Some beaders will even swap beads with other beaders via the world wide web. There are even bead auctions on line. When you bid on these beads or stones from an auction you wait anxiously to see if you will win , then you wait anxiously to receive them. Wow! I challenge you to shop on line, you will thank me later.

Bead Shows, Bead Festivals, Bead Swap Meets, Bead Cruises, Bead Socials, and more are all good shopping sources. They are held all around the United States. Be prepared for a treat. The sponsors work very hard to make each event extraordinary. You can truly "shop till you drop". They are awesome because so many vendors participate and you get to meet other Beadaholiques! The last Festival I attended consisted of over three hundred vendors. So imagine having that many stores all under one roof, each displaying their best beads. I found it very hard to leave. There were hands on workshops offered too, which were reasonably priced. This is why most of the shows last two or three days. Can you imagine staying in a hotel hosting a bead show? With that many beads stores right below you, sleep deprivation is sure to set in and bead dreams would be inevitable.

NO MATTER WHICH SHOPPING SOURCE I USE AFTERWARDS I'M TOO ANXIOUS TO GET MY BEAD ON!

ATTENTION!   **ATTENTION!**   **ATTENTION!**   **ATTENTION!**

Just in From the Newsroom at BETRUE NEWS

Citrine Quartz Reporting: A young woman has just been escorted out of the Craftmania Store by the Bead Patrol. She remained in the isle containing precious and semi-precious stones after several announcements were made to bring all purchases to the cashier. Closing time had lapsed by fifteen minutes.

When approached by two Bead Patrol Agents and asked to leave once again, she began to cry and yell "I can't leave you beads. I want to take you all home with me". The Bead Patrol Agents had to place her into beaded bangle bracelets to calm her down. She was then escorted to the Beadmobile en route to Beadville Sanitarium, where she will be evaluated and possibly B02ed.

Reporting to you live, this is Citrine Quartz back to the Newsroom at Betrue News

Reporter Amber Amethyst: There seems to be a new awareness involving beads. They are showing up everywhere. More and more people are coming forward, confessing their need to bead! Some say there is a beadbug going around. It has something to do with stringing and blinging ordinary items with stones, glass, metal and several other beaded materials. This young woman is one of many escorted from a craft store in this manner during the past few weeks. There may be a bead revolution beginning. We must mention that this bead arrest was a little different because this beadster had theme music repeating over and over: beadbug take me away playing from her mp3 player while being carried away.

This is Amber Amethyst reporting from the Newsroom at Betrue News. We will keep you updated on the outcome of this story.

JUST BEAD IT

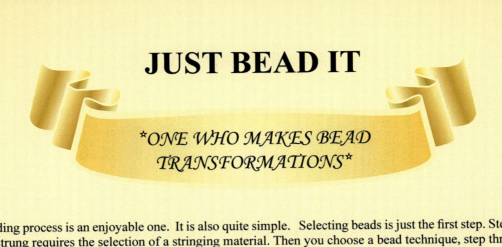

ONE WHO MAKES BEAD TRANSFORMATIONS

The beading process is an enjoyable one. It is also quite simple. Selecting beads is just the first step. Step two, getting those beads strung requires the selection of a stringing material. Then you choose a bead technique, step three.

Just Bead It will be an experiment. We'll place three beaders at a table and give each of them the same focal bead (the main bead in a design) and let's say about six trays of complimentary beads. Provide the same stringing material for all three. Then instruct each one to design a bracelet. You will see that each beaded strand will be different from the next one.

Beaders can mix it up and produce awesome finished creations. This is why thousands of beaded designs exist in the world and more are being produced each time someone tries beading. Each design has its own uniqueness that comes from the designer. I have created several hundred designs myself, no two are the same. It is very easy to change the look of a design just by changing one bead or a group of beads in the original pattern. You can also change the look of a design by changing the stringing material. Instead of string, use leather cord. Then try the same design using wire mesh or fabric cord. Some beaders use other craft techniques like bead crochet, bead knitting, and bead weaving to design some of the flattering creations we see.

Step one, step two, step three and here begins Beadalousity. Beads, beads, and more beads! Bead makers are dedicated to making beautiful beads to string. They use some usual and some unusual materials. I would like to applaud all those who make or manufacture any kind of bead. Yeah! Because of you, I don't have to worry about making beads right now. Because of you, I can stick to stringing the beads I have and before I finish with them you have created new ones. By the way, I found some strange bead types out there after attending a craft show. Beads are being made out of materials I won't mention. Imagine that?

The chart below mentions only twelve of each bead type that I will categorize as usual and unusual beads.

THE USUAL	Glass	Crystal	Silver	Gold	Copper	Plastic
	Paper	Wire	Metal	Wood	Polymer Clay	Silver Clay

THE UNUSUAL	Buttons	Bottle Caps	Knobs	Compact Discs	Records	Tassels
	Cording	Keys	Camera Parts	Resin	Coins	Fabric

The next Just Bead It experiment is to create a design out of each one of materials mentioned above. Start with the unusual category. You probably have most of these things right in your home. In the meantime, I want to share another beadaholique moment.

I went to a fabric store in my hometown. This store has a reputation for having very exclusive fabric. While browsing over the many bulks of fabric; I saw a light blue cotton/silk blend with metallic thread running through it. This fabric made me want to run home to my sewing machine and start sewing. I bought several yards to do just that. Yes, I sew too! Sewing is in third position on the list of crafts I enjoy, right after painting on tee shirts. Of course beading is in first place. The garment I chose, a blouse, turned out great! When I thought about accessorizing the blouse, it occurred to me that I could make beads out of fabric. Well I did just that. This fabric got into my way and became a bead. Fabric beads are a definite way to compliment an outfit. Blouses with matching necklace and earrings may become a new fashion statement. My ensemble is featured on the back cover. This is another example of Beadalousity: unlimited beaded imagination. Beads and bead bling always makes a statement, complimenting an outfit just like:

ICING ON A CAKE

FUDGE ON A SUNDAE

CHERRIES ON TOP OF A CHEESECAKE

WHIPPED CREAM ON PANCAKES

STRAWBERRIES ON TOP OF WAFFLES

SPRINKLES ON TOP OF AN ICE CREAM CONE

I must stop! Now I don't know whether I want to bead or binge?

Now beside the usual and unusual types of beads, there are special ones called Gemstones. They hide within the earth's matter and must be discovered. Gemstones are mentioned in the Holy Bible as far back as the days of Moses. In the Book of Exodus, the Breastplate worn by the Jewish High Priest is adorned with gemstones, gold and linen. Many believe the roots of birthstones began during this time. Each month of the calendar year has a gemstone/birthstone that corresponds with it. Everyone has a birthstone. I have provided a chart in case you do not know yours. Each of these stones represent natural beauty without effort which is a quality of human beings. Have you discovered your natural beauty?

January Garnet	February Amethyst	March Aquamarine	April Diamond
May Emerald	June Pearl	July Ruby	August Peridot
September Sapphire	October Opal	November Citrine	December Blue Topaz

LIVE FROM BETRUE NEWS:

We interrupt your enjoyment through the pages of this book to report this update:

Citrine Quartz Reporting: We are here with the Chief of Staff at Beadville Sanitarium, Dr. Ruby Garnet.

Dr. Garnet have you evaluated the young woman brought in by the Bead Patrol from Craftmania on yesterday?

Dr. Garnet: Yes Citrine, we have. The young lady's name is Beadella Bluestone. She is a native of Rocky Mountain Pennsylvania. Ms. Bluestone is experiencing a touch of what we at Beadville call Stage I Beadbug. She also meets the criteria for Beadaholiqueism. Although there is no known cure treatment is available.

Citrine: Dr. Garnet; Is Ms. Bluestone a threat to herself or others?

Dr. Garnet: Ms. Bluestone does not pose a threat to herself or others. As a matter of fact She has been very content in her private room decorated with the latest in beaded accessories. She no longer requires the use of beaded bangle bracelets to calm her. Our goal is to keep her mind focused on one bead project at a time. This is one of the common practices we use for a patient beginning B.N.A.(Beadaholique Non Anonymous) recovery. Her passion is on overload so she must be treated gently.

Citrine: Would you elaborate more about the treatments that are available?

Dr. Garnet: Our facility is fully equipped with craft rooms complete with the latest bead ingredients needed to make the finest designs she can imagine. Our expert instructors are also here to assist Ms. Bluestone in her time of need.

Citrine: Her time of need?

Dr. Garnet: Yes, she just needs to bead. We will place her on a temporary schedule to help her better allocate the time she spends beading and monitor her closely.

Citrine: One final question Dr. Garnet; Will Ms. Bluestone face any criminal charges?

Dr. Garnet: After release from our facility, she will have to report to Judge Jade Jewelstone to determine if any criminal charges are in order.

Citrine: What are her chances? Everyone in the bead world knows Judge Jewelstone is a stringing Judge.

Dr. Garnet: If Ms. Bluestone allows us to help her with controlling her passion, she should be ok.

Citrine: Thank you for your bead up on this story Dr. Garnet. This is Citrine Quartz reporting from Beadville Sanitarium where Ms. Beadella Bluestone is recovering from Stage I Beadbug. We will continue to keep you updated on this story. Back to the newsroom

BACK AT BETRUE NEWS

Amber Amethyst: The phone lines here at BETRUE NEWS have been ringing off the hook with questions about this story. Although we cannot answer them all, the most frequently asked is: "Is Beadbug contagious?" We intend to get the answer to this question at the next interview.

So stay tuned!

IF THE TRUTH BE TOLD, YOU GOT IT FROM BETRUE NEWS!

CRAFT CRAZE

I have been a crafter since childhood. There are several memories I recall that helped spark my crafting desires. I remember when my father wanted to open a retail jewelry business: "Steve's Gifts". With six children, an assembly line seemed to be a sure way to get those necklaces and earrings made at low cost. We all sat at the table with a specific task. Laughing and talking is what we did as we worked. We enjoyed ourselves so much it seemed like play not work. Sometimes we used a timer to see how fast we could reach Daddy's quota. This made the work seem more like play. So I fondly reflect on those sessions as our personal bead parties!

Aunt Marie, was my father's sister. I am told that I was named after her because of the freckles on my nose just like hers. When my parents let me spend weekends with her, she would share her craftiness with me by letting me help her with whatever project she was working on at that time. Most of the time it was floral arranging but she made jewelry too.

I also attribute my craftiness to the Helping Hand Mission right across the street from where we lived. This Mission still stands today. You had to participate in Bible study in order to join an arts and craft club. I chose the sewing club. Because of this club I was able to make my own clothes to wear to school. I participated in other craft clubs too. The instructors who volunteered their time to the Mission were students from various colleges all around the city. They were so kind and patient with the neighborhood children. Believe me we were no angels but they always planned a good time for everybody. We went on field trips that gave us a chance to see places outside the inner city. That's when I got my first glimpse of mountains. Mountains are where many precious stones are found. Hurray for mountains. My siblings and I always made sure our chores were done so we could go to the Mission. When we were not at the Mission we went to the Friends Neighborhood Guild, another place where we could participate in activities, learn crafts and get help with our homework.

Several years ago I became interested in earrings made with wire. Hoop shaped earrings made with 14 karat gold-filled beads on gold wire were in style then. The demand was off the chain! I could not make enough of them. I was even repairing items made by other designers. The demand slowed down as the fad became less popular. Working with those beads was great. Thus, my wire working skills evolved.

Back in 2002, I went to visit my brother Nate and his wife Tonya on the beautiful Island of Hawaii. My youngest brother Mark was there too. After the first two weeks of touring and sampling the native food, my sister-in-law decided to take me to a bead show right on the Island. It was my first! If you had to comment on my actions at this event you would have said she was like a child in Disneyland. I will say I was like an adult in Beadland or Beadworld. There is a Disneyworld too. I developed a craving for this world of beads. So the next day, we visited one of the craft stores on the Island called Bella's Beads. A Paradise (Bella's Beads) was within a Paradise (Hawaii). When I entered this store, I had to take a few deep breaths. The displays within this store were breathtaking.   The owner personally welcomed me to her store and to the Island. Bella did not just sell beading supplies and materials she taught classes right in her shop. Right away I selected a class titled: "Flower Garden Bracelet".   The class would teach me a wire wrapping technique using 20 gauge wire, seed beads, and flower beads in different colors. To my surprise and disappointment the class was full. When Bella realized I was visiting she offered to teach me the technique one-on-one. I wanted to start the class right away.

After receiving that special one-on-one session, I bought a bunch of supplies to practice my newly learned skill. I might have gone a little seed bead crazy. Seed beads are the smallest bead of them all. They come in hundreds of colors. When I got back to the house, I began to make a few bracelets on my own. When I finished the third one Tonya came over to check on me. She immediately said, "Sis you are really outdoing yourself!" We have to go back to the bead store and show Bella. The next day we did just that. Bella was amazed! She shook her head and said: "I should never have taught you". We all laughed yet the laughter continues because I have not stopped beading to this day. I am forever grateful to Bella. Thank you for the special attention.

By the way, I named my technique "Hawaiian Bracelet". There are no flower beads on my revised creations but plenty of seed beads. It is exciting to see how different they look one from the other although I used the same basic technique. I also tried the same technique to make a pennant and matching earrings.

As I have mentioned before, craft shows are a good place to shop for beading supplies and materials. After reading this chapter, you will know they are also a great place to spark your lack of enthusiasm. I will even take matters a bit further and say Your bbd (bad bead day) will turn into a gbd (good bead day) if you attend a craft show, festival, bead party, bead cruise or retreat. I have compared my bead adventures to Disneyworld in Orlando, Florida. I recall not wanting to leave that place either, my son and I were having too much fun. These bead affairs are social events that beaders and nonbeaders can enjoy. An experience that you will not forget.

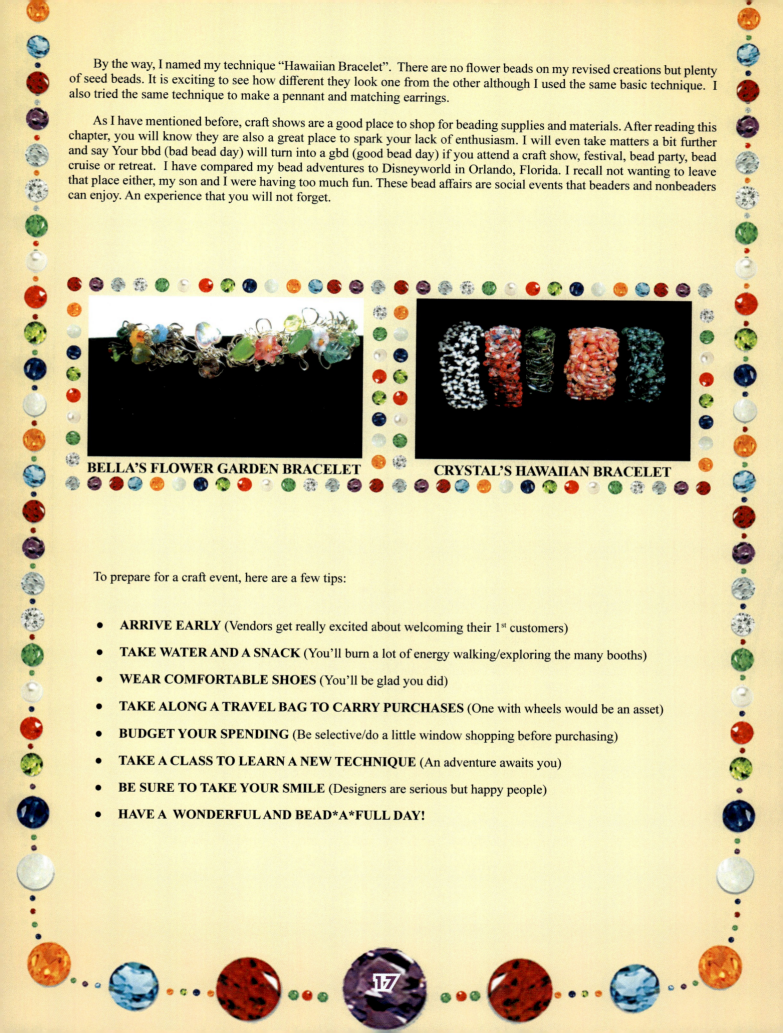

BELLA'S FLOWER GARDEN BRACELET   **CRYSTAL'S HAWAIIAN BRACELET**

To prepare for a craft event, here are a few tips:

- **ARRIVE EARLY** (Vendors get really excited about welcoming their 1st customers)

- **TAKE WATER AND A SNACK** (You'll burn a lot of energy walking/exploring the many booths)

- **WEAR COMFORTABLE SHOES** (You'll be glad you did)

- **TAKE ALONG A TRAVEL BAG TO CARRY PURCHASES** (One with wheels would be an asset)

- **BUDGET YOUR SPENDING** (Be selective/do a little window shopping before purchasing)

- **TAKE A CLASS TO LEARN A NEW TECHNIQUE** (An adventure awaits you)

- **BE SURE TO TAKE YOUR SMILE** (Designers are serious but happy people)

- **HAVE A WONDERFUL AND BEAD*A*FULL DAY!**

We are back! Live from Beadville Sanitarium. Where Dr. Garnet will allow a face to face interview with Ms. Bluestone

Citrine: Good Morning Ms. Bluestone. How are you feeling today and what's going on?

Ms. Bluestone: Good Morning Citrine. I'm feeling great! First I want to thank everyone for their concern. My name is Beadella but my friends call me Beadsz.

I am a Beadaholique! I confess it. To my beads I will be true! The episode I experienced the other day was not abnormal for those who are involved with beading. I saw so many wonderful stones or beads as we call them, I just did not hear any announcements being made. The next thing I knew I was being escorted out by the Bead Patrol. They say I refused to leave. I say that I was not ready, willing or able to leave. I get into this mood sometimes.

Dr. Garnet: That's why we care here at Beadville. We know there is no cure for her Beadbug and it is contagious. When a patient is exposed their recovery excels as they become more exposed. She is only here to gain knowledge on how to properly nourish her condition. Ms. Bluestone is creating quite a fuss in this facility too. Her creative juices flow through every class. She wants to master every technique we offer.

Beadsz: The people here are fantastic. They understand my passion. I want to be the best beader I can be. The staff here is the best so I am receiving the best care available. I will face Judge Jewelstone tomorrow. I will make my plea, then go right back to being me: Beadsz.

Citrine: Are you afraid there might be a stiff sentence?

Beadsz: No way! The Judge can't touch me. I'm full of life and beadalousity. I've even written a book all about it. The book explains everything in detail.

Dr. Garnet: Now Beadsz let's not get too excited. We want you to be ready for the Judge tomorrow.

Beadsz: Yes Dr. Garnet; but I want everyone to know I believe in beads. I have no fear. I'm ready to face tomorrow but while I have today, I'll just bead.

Citrine: There you have it fellow Beadsters. Your beloved Beadsz is doing just fine. I guess we can find her book at a local bookstore so we can get the bead up on this one. I am on my way to get my copy now! Back to the Newsroom.

Newsroom at BETRUE News

Amber: The phone lines are slowly dying down. I guess the fans are on their way to the bookstore. Hope they keep late hours. I don't know if there is a Book Patrol but no one can own too many books. I hope Citrine picks up a few copies of Beadsz's book for us.

That's a rap for now! We'll have front row seats in the Courtroom tomorrow. Until then signing off with the beadbug song. (song in background) Beadbug take me away. Beadbug take me away.

BEADOLOGY 101

(Required course for all Beadville patients)

Happy Beadday

Happy Beadday to you!
Happy Beadday to you!
Happy Beadday…..ay!
Happy Beadday…..ay!
Happy Beadday to you!

They say it's true
If you string one, you're through
Ahead are great beading days
So come what may!

From Beadsz

TO BEAD OR NOT TO BEAD

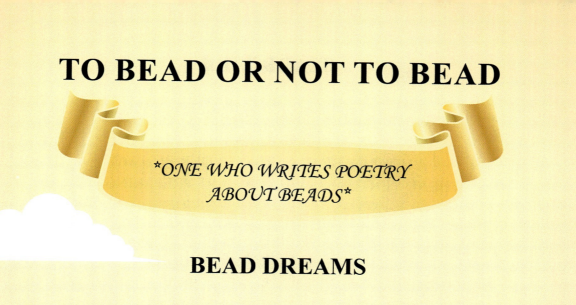

ONE WHO WRITES POETRY ABOUT BEADS

BEAD DREAMS

WOKE UP THIS MORNING WITH BEADS ON MY MIND
MY HANDS WERE READY, A CLEAR SPACE WAS NEAR
I EVEN JUGGLED MY TIME
I FOUND A NEW WAY TO EASE MY FRUSTRATION
THESE BEADS THAT POSSESS ME, THEY DESIRE FORMATION
SO HAPPILY DOWN THE BEAD'IN PATH I GO
WITH A ROAD MAP OF VISION, PATIENCE AND DETERMINATION
TO FINISH MY TASK
GATHERING A FEW PRECIOUS STONES, GLASS RONDELLS, SEED BEADS,
SILVER, GOLD, AND COPPER TOO
A CRYSTAL BEAD HERE, CRAFT WIRE THERE AND
MY TOOLS SHARP AND SHINED, EACH KNOW WHAT TO DO
MY NEW FOUND PASSION; IT COULD BE LOVE
JUST TOOK A ROUTE OF ITS OWN
IF I'M DREAMING, PLEASE DON'T WAKE ME UP
I'LL JUST CLICK MY HEELS TO GET HOME
LOOK! MY DESIGN IS COMPLETE
I'M TICKLED PINK
IMAGINE A THOUGHT PROCESSED THEN TRANSFORMED
HAS NOW BECOME MY CREATION
READY TO PRESENT TO THE WHOLE WIDE WORLD
A BEADED FASHION SENSATION

BEADBOARD

BEADBOARD BEADBOARD PLEASE BE STILL
TOOLS ARE AT YOUR SIDE
A HOST OF BEADS ARE ON YOUR RUNWAY
A BEAD VENTURE IS WHAT WE ARE PREPARING FOR
SO GET READY FOR THE RIDE

SEATBELT FASTENED…. HOLD ON TIGHT
THERE IS NO WRONG OR RIGHT
WITH THE HELP OF YOUR SURFACE AND YOUR GROOVES
THIS RIDE IS SURE TO BE DARING YET SMOOTH

QUALITY TIME WILL HAVE TO COUNT
ESTIMATED TIME OF ARRIVAL IS UNSURE
SO WHAT WE ACCOMPLISH IN THE END
WILL BE A WORK OF ART AND…….MORE

BEADBOARD: I KNOW THIS TRIP WILL EVENTUALLY END
YOU WILL BE HERE FROM BEGINNING TO END
SO WHEN I FINISH MY MASTERPIECE

I'LL REALIZE…………….

I TRAVELED WITH A FRIEND

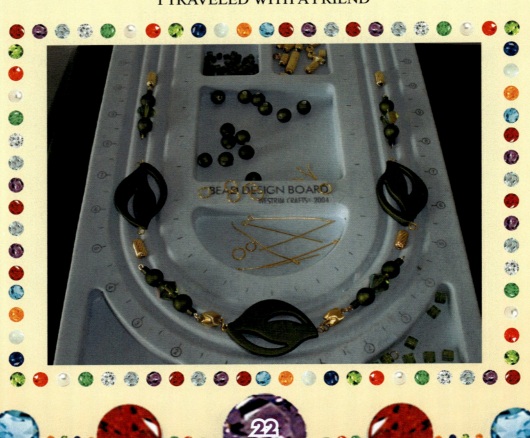

TOOLS

TOOLS ARE USED TO ASSEMBLE OUR DESIGNS

SO BEADERS PLEASE TAKE HEED

THE CORRECT USE OF EACH IS THE KEY

TO A FINISHED PIECE OF BEADED JEWELRY

SO COME ROUNDNOSE PLIERS

COME CHAINNOSE PLIERS

COME BENTNOSE PLIERS TOO

LEARNING THEIR NAMES ARE IMPORTANT

EACH ONE HAS A CHORE TO DO

SO COME SPLITRING PLIERS

COME CRIMPERS

WIRE CUTTERS SURELY WITHOUT YOU

OUR GOALS WOULD BE UNREACHABLE

LIKE A CROSSWORD WITHOUT A CLUE

COLOR WHEEL

COLOR WHEEL GOOD MORNING!
YOU BRIGHTEN UP MY DAY
WITH THE CONTINUOUS RAINBOW
OF COLOR HUES
THAT YOU SEND MY WAY

I CAN ONLY IMAGINE YOUR BEGINNING
I'M UNSURE OF WHERE YOU END
SO WHEN I ROTATE AROUND YOUR AXIS
NEW IDEAS, WITHIN MY MIND, ALSO SPIN

COLOR WHEEL THANK YOU!
YOU INSPIRE ME! WITH YOUR:
ROSEY REDS
MELLOW YELLOWS
COOL PINKS
GARDEN GREENS
PASSIONATE PURPLES
AWESOME ORANGES
BLOSSOMING BLUES
BOLD BLACKS
GRACEFUL GRAYS
AND WINTER WHITES TOO
WITH YOU MY DEAR COLOR WHEEL
BEADING WILL NEVER BE BORING OR BLUE

This poem is dedicated to all men who share a passion for beading.

BEAD MEN

MEN WHO BEAD WANT TO SET THE RECORD STRAIGHT

ALL THIS TALK ABOUT STONES IS GREAT

A CAVE MAN WOULD BE PROUD

INSTEAD OF DRAGGING THAT STONE AROUND, HE COULD FINALLY LAY IT DOWN

HE COULD <u>HAMMER AND CHISEL</u> IT IN THE MORNING

HE COULD <u>WAX, BUFF AND SHINE</u> IT THAT AFTERNOON

HE COULD DRILL <u>A HOLE IN ONE</u> IN THE EVENING

THEN LET HIS <u>CHEST SET</u> OUT ALL NIGHT

JEWELRY

J is for **JEWELRY**

THE MEDIAN THROUGH WHICH MY GIFT IS REPRESENTED

E is for ENERGY

RELEASED IN THE MAKING OF EACH DESIGN

W is for WISDOM

REQUESTED AND RECEIVED FROM ABOVE

E is for EXPRESSION

RELEASED THROUGH PRECIOUS STONES

L is for LIFE

SO WONDERFUL SO FULL SO SWEET

R is for REALITY

KNOWING WHAT YOU CHOOSE TO ACCOMPLISH

BECOMES REAL WHEN YOU REFUSE TO ACCEPT DEFEAT

Y is for YES

YES I CAN BE ALL THAT I CAN BE! BECAUSE

MY TASK IS COMPLETE FOR ALL THE WORLD TO SEE

This next poem is an adventure all by itself. I love going to the back of my bead magazines just to experience the creativity unleashed using a bead prefix. If I owned a beadstore it would be called BEADMANIA, BEADVILLE or STONE CRAZY. I have imagined traveling to bead stores, meeting the owners and clientele who may be stone bead crazy too. Imagine Beadsz showing up in your town in a Beadmobile. Oh well, anything is possible! Here we go down The Beaded Path

THE BEADED PATH

Step by Step   Stone by Stone   I traveled under   A Beaded Moon   down

A Beaded Path   with   My Bead Basket   full of   Bead Treasures

through   A Beaded Gate   entering   A Bead Paradise   flourishing   with

A Bead Garden   that contained   A Bead Tree   next to   A Bead Bungalow

shaped like   A Bead Hive   full of   Bead Bugs   chatting the latest   Bead Biz

about the next   Bead Bazaar   held at   The Bead Hall of Fame   honoring

The Bead Queen   who shares her   Beadtopia   of   Bead Dreams   and fulfills

Any Bead Need   by granting   A Bead Bath and Beyond   filled with

A Bead Cache   from the   Bead Bar None   tons of fun!   Then I will   Boldly Bead

right to her   Beadoir   which is more like   A Bead Boutique   full of   Bead Styles

that are creatively   Bead Unique   like this   Bead Quest   where   The Bead Goes On

finally yet importantly   All Beads Aboard   don't forget your   Bead and Button

we are going to   Bead Away!

MY MAILBOX

I confess that when I go to my mailbox and there is a bead magazine, bead book or a post card advertising a bead event it helps make my day. Imagine as I slowly approach my mailbox. It is filled with bills, advertisements, junk mail, cards, etc. Then to my surprise, a bead magazine lies in the midst of the pile. My eyes began to glow, my teeth began to show and I start singing: "I got a bead magazine, I got a bead magazine". I look at the cover and read the captions listing the bead feast that I will enjoy. By now my heart is beating a little faster. I must take deep breaths or bead anxiety may take over. That's just beadbug in an acute stage. I want to browse these pages right away but I hold back. My magazine will be my late night read. Waiting until bedtime to read its contents increases my chances of dreaming about the contents and waking up the next morning with fresh ideas. Most magazines contain one hundred pages or more so it takes some time to reach the end. The more nights I spend with it, makes reading it more enjoyable. You must indulge one. You will be amazed. I have a favorite but I truly enjoy every one I read. I am glad I have my bead magazine subscriptions (now you know I have more than one). They make going to the mailbox a trip I look forward to every day. I truly consider them a treat: Allow me to entice your bead appetite while I have your attention:

The Cover: Always so colorful with jewelry designs beaming from the page, aah……ah

A host of headlines of what's inside are plastered all over the cover too.

The Table of Contents: Tells me the exact page to find the projects I want to feast on.

The Editors Notes: Make me feel like I'm reading a letter from a friend. The editor speaks bead language. When I want to write back and I can use e-mail, text, blogs, live chats or a good old fashion letter.

Comments from other Readers: As if sharing with the editor is not satisfying enough, how about hearing from hundreds of other beaders speaking bead language too!

The Main Course: The jewelry design featured on the cover is like a main course. It comes with complete instructions. You get a list of the supplies you need and pictures to help walk you through each step. I have tried a few new techniques using the illustrations in my magazines. They help me keep up with the latest trends and styles although jewelry designs rarely go out of style.

(Food for Thought - Vintage jewelry is still around so jewelry styles come and go and come again.)

Advertisements: I used to think some magazines had too many ads, but not anymore. You see one day I decided to just explore all the ads in one of my bead magazines. There were ads from importers, manufacturers, wholesalers, retailers, individuals, bead shows, bead festivals, bead talk shows, bead auctioneers, bead societies, bead cruise lines and more. No one listed any invites to a bead party yet so I guess I'll have to host my own some day. Advertisments introduce the new beading tools that are available and new beads that are on the scene. Just reading the creative names that bead companies use **rock** my bead world. Bead magazines also have websites.

The Websites: If you dare to go online get ready! get ready! get ready! A bead venture online can surely blow your mind along with your time! Warning: I take no responsibility for the time you spend on your bead adventure through the world wide web. I would not have access to so many stores if I didn't subscribe to the magazines that list websites that represent my craft. There are hundreds, maybe thousands but each one I visit makes me want to have one of my own. A website will be my next venture. My fellow beaders will probably want to keep up with a confessed Beadaholique's work.

Bead Books: My sister-in-law Tonya is so sweet and she helps feed my bead needs. She has been sending me bead books in the mail for several years. Therefore, when that package (a bead book) comes in the mail it is like receiving a birthday present. I have a different song for that day, Happy Beadday To You. I wrote a bead version of this song for beaders. Some bead magazines I subscribe to list the latest bead book releases. The descriptions they give help me choose which ones to order. I order at least two books on my own yearly. Bead books are the greatest. They contain pages and pages dedicated to those things that make stuff bling.

Post Cards: Small but important, I must mention these. When there is a bead event or the opening of a new bead store in my area there is usually a postcard in my mailbox to let me know the date and location. Occasionally the larger shows that are in other states send announcements by postcard too. Their arrival means a vacation may be in order.

I HOPE YOUR EXPERIENCE WITH MY BEAD MAIL HAS BEEN INTERESTING AND INFORMATIVE. I CANNOT WAIT UNTIL THIS BOOK IS FINISHED. I INTEND TO HAVE A COPY SENT TO ME BY UPS, FEDERAL EXPRESS AND PONY EXPRESS. I WILL EVEN REQUEST A COPY SENT TO ME THROUGH THE UNITED STATES POSTAL SYSTEM VIA EXPRESS MAIL SPECIAL DELIVERY. MOVE OVER BILLS!

I GOT MY BOOK IN THE MAIL! I GOT MY BOOK IN THE MAIL!

ATTENTION!   **ATTENTION!**   **ATTENTION!**   **ATTENTION!**

Reporting live from the Rock Solid Courthouse in Rocky Mountain PA., This is Amber Amethyst reporting (Citrine is at home reading Beadsz's Book) Order has been called so let's listen in:

Judge Jade Jewelstone: Ms. Bluestone you have been sworn to tell the truth, the whole truth and nothing but the truth, correct?

Beadella Bluestone: Yes your Honor

Judge Jewelstone: Ms. Bluestone you have been charged with the following:

1. Disorderly Conduct

2. Deviant Trespassing, resulting in delayed closing of the store known as Craftmania

3. Filling a basket full of precious and semi-precious stones that had to be restocked

4. Spreading an epidemic of Beadbug.

5. Causing craft stores and this courtroom to be full of bead designers, bead makers, bead stringers, beadaholiques and other bead kinds

How do you plead?

Ms. Bluestone: Guilty Your Honor

Judge Jewelstone: Do you have representation?

Attorney Silver: Your Honor Attorney Sterling Silver here on behalf of Ms. Bluestone. My client is a very talented young woman who has a passion for the craft of beading. If it would please the court, the people would like to call: Dr. Ruby Garnet. She is the physician that evaluated Ms. Bluestone's condition while at Beadville Sanitarium.

Judge Jewelstone: Please swear in the Doctor.

Attorney Silver: Dr. Garnet will you please tell the Court your diagnosis of Ms. Bluestone's condition.

Dr. Garnet: Ms. Bluestone, affectionately known to us at Beadville as Beadsz, is a Beadaholique who has experienced an outbreak of stage I Beadbug. The symptoms consist of but are not limited to an overindulgence of her desire for beads. The patient desires to acquire every bead that she sees. Therefore shopping for them becomes addictive at times. She has responded very well to treatment at our facility. Her compulsive behavior has been redirected with the help of our special Psychobeadopathy treatments. Most patients with this type of disorder have a creative nature that is limitless if shown the right direction.

Beadville is a Haven designed for such patients. A place that allows them to bond with others who understand their needs while learning new coping techniques. We therefore recommend that she be released under her own will and allowed to continue creating her beautiful handcrafted beaded designs. My report provides full details of her condition and subsequent treatment.

Judge Jewelstone: (Judge looks at report). Tell me Dr. Garnet if this patient is a threat to herself or society?

Dr. Garnet: The only threat she poses Your Honor is sharing her abundant, enthusiastic love for beads.

Attorney Silver: My client is sorry for any inconvenience she may have caused the staff at Craftmania Your Honor

Judge Jewelstone: Very well, Ms. Bluestone aka Beadsz

(Audience chants she's not crazy she's Beadsz!). (The Judge slams her gavel)

Silence in this Courtroom! As I was about to say: Ms Bluestone you have pleaded guilty to the charges listed. You have received treatment but the court is not completely satisfied with just releasing you as a Beadaholique experiencing Beadbug; therefore I order you to:

Submit a signed copy of the Beader's Creed to the court

Submit ten of your original bead designs, which will later become exhibits at the Craftmania store

Make your favorite tee shirt designs available to your new fans (Courtroom observers cheer!)

Last but not least, You must volunteer fifteen hours of community service to the Craftmania store

You may personally sign copies of your book during this time and discuss the contents

Report back to me in thirty days. Court adjourned. (Judge slams gavel)

Amber: Well Beadsz fans, looks like we are going to get quite a few treats! A look at the Beader's Creed, a preview of Ms. Bluestone's beadedmania, beaded designer tee shirts and an opportunity to meet her personally. This Judge really knows how to string things along! I don't know about you but I want my book signed by Beadsz and my tee shirt order filled ASAP.

Back to the Newsroom at BETRUE News

CREATIONS BY BEADSZ

The Beaders Creed

(Must be recited holding a bead, stone or charm in hand)

The Beaders Creed

I AM A BEADAHOLIQUE

I DO HEREBY PROMISE TO COMMIT

TO THE CRAFT OF BEADING

TO STRING ANY BEAD I CHOOSE TO THE BEST OF MY ABILITY

TO HONOR THE SPIRIT, ENTHUSIASM AND SATISFACTION THAT ACCOMPANIES BEADING

TO DELIGHT IN MY CRAFT BY LEARNING NEW TECHNIQUES

I WILL RESPECT THE ORIGINAL DESIGNS OF MY FELLOW BEADERS

I WILL ALWAYS STRIVE TO FINISH ANY PROJECT I START

I WILL NEVER ENTER ANY TWELVE STEP PROGRAM

DESIGNED TO RELINQUISH MY NEED TO BEAD

KNOWING THAT BEADERS ARE A SPECIAL BREED OF THE MANY VARIETIES OF CRAFTERS

I WILL TO MY BEADS BE TRUE!

Signature *BEADSZ*

EXHIBITS

Shellissa

ONE

GARDEN IN BRONZE

TWO

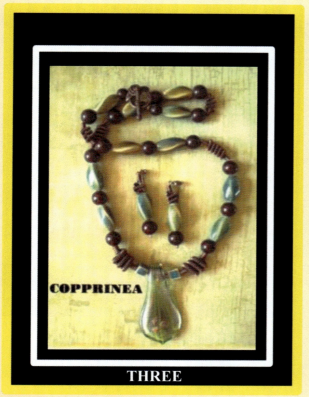

COPPRINEA

THREE

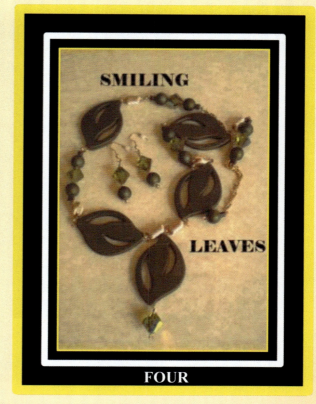

SMILING LEAVES

FOUR

33

ISLAND MELODY

FIVE

STONEMAZING

SIX

CRANBERRY PEARLS

SEVEN

PEARISHA

EIGHT

ONE SPIRAL WAY

NINE

IRRADESSA

TEN

Judge's Summary of Beadsz's Submissions

Judge Jade Jewelstone: I have examined the items ordered by this court to be submitted by Ms. Beadella Bluestone aka Beadsz. She has expressed her commitment to beading by signing a copy of the Beader's Creed.

Her designs exhibit a creative style of her very own by way of the bead varieties used, her tasteful use of colors, as well as necklace and earring combinations that are uniquely one of a kind. Her passion for the craft of beading shows through her work.

Her tee shirts can be proudly worn by anyone. The designs are inspirational. I especially like her tee shirt with the slogan BEAD PEACE with a peace sign, which she wore to court.

The Craftmania store was very pleased with the extra publicity and sales they received during her hours of community service, therefore they are going to express their appreciation by hosting a bead party in Beadsz's honor immediately after this summation. Everyone is invited!

Beadsz all charges against you are hereby dismissed. This Court wants to encourage you to keep doing what you do, creating beautiful beaded designs and being you. Remember the skills you learned at Beadville and you will not have to return to this Courtroom. Happy Beadday to You! Court adjourned!

SING A BEAD SONG

ONE WHO WRITES SONGS ABOUT BEADS

BEAD BUG (The Song)

This song is dedicated to Lil. Ernie Jr. My Bead Bug!

BEAD BUG TAKE ME AWAY BEAD BUG TAKE ME AWAY

I NEED YOUR LOVE TODAY SO BEAD BUG TAKE ME AWAY

BEAD BUG TAKE ME AWAY BEAD BUG TAKE ME AWAY

I NEED YOUR LOVE TODAY SO BEAD BUG TAKE ME AWAY

THERE IS A BEAD THEY SAY THAT GETS IN THE WAY

YOU CAN START FROM THE THE LEFT OR THE RIGHT

NO MATTER WHAT YOU DO ITS TOTALLY UP TO YOU

BUT WATCH OUT! THE BEAD BUG WILL BITE!

BEAD BUG TAKE ME AWAY BEAD BUG TAKE ME AWAY

I NEED YOUR LOVE TODAY SO BEAD BUG TAKE ME AWAY

BEAD BUG TAKE ME AWAY BEAD BUG TAKE ME AWAY

I NEED YOUR LOVE TODAY SO BEAD BUG TAKE ME AWAY

GIVE ME a B. **B** GIVE ME an E. **E** GIVE ME an A. **A** GIVE ME a D. **D**

AND a **B** AND a **U** AND a **G** YEAH BEAD BUG TAKE ME AWAY

(REPEAT)

BEAD BUG... TAKE ME... AWAY... BEAD BUG!

"YOU'RE STONE CRAZY" *(THE SONG)*

CHORUS: YOU'RE STONE CRAZY GIRL IN A STONE CRAZY WORLD (REPEAT 2x)

VERSE ONE: EVERYBODY TAKE HEED

THIS SONGS ABOUT THE BEAD

YOU SEE I'VE GOT THIS NEED

I JUST NEED TO BEAD!

CHORUS: YOU'RE STONE CRAZY GIRL IN A STONE CRAZY WORLD (REPEAT 2x)

VERSE TWO: IT'S THE CRAFT I CHOOSE

IT'S LIKE BUYING SHOES

I CAN'T BUY ENOUGH I CAN'T KEEP HUSH HUSH

YOU SEE BEADS AND ME, SPELL BEADALOSITY

CHORUS: YOU'RE STONE CRAZY GIRL IN A STONE CRAZY WORLD (REPEAT 2x)

VERSE THREE: IT'S PLAIN TO SEE

A BEAD QUEEN, THAT'S ME

I'M FULL OF LIFE AND CREATIVITY

CHORUS: YOU'RE STONE CRAZY GIRL IN A STONE CRAZY WORLD (REPEAT 2x)

VERSE FOUR: I DON'T WANT TO BOAST I TRAVELED COAST TO COAST

TO SEEK AND FIND WHAT'S JUST STONES TO MOST

WENT AROUND THE WORLD JUST TO FIND A PEARL

WENT TO TANZEEN THERE I FOUND CITRINE

WHEN I FOUND THE BEAD THE ONE THAT FILLED MY NEEDS

IT WAS INSIDE OF ME, IT WAS A SEED BEAD

CHORUS: YOU'RE STONE CRAZY GIRL IN A STONE CRAZY WORLD (REPEAT 2x)

(BEAT CHANGE) CHORUS: NOW GET YOUR BEAD ON GIRL (REPEAT 3x)

I CAN BEAD ALL DAY

I CAN BEAD ALL NIGHT

IF YOU TOUCH MY BEADS

YOU MIGHT HAVE TO FIGHT

I CAN BEAD IN THE SUNSHINE

BEAD IN THE RAIN

DRY MYSELF OFF AND START BEADING AGAIN

CHORUS: YOUR'RE STONE CRAZY GIRL IN A STONE CRAZY WORLD

(REPEAT UNTIL END OF SONG)

THE B.E.A.D. ~ END

ONE WHO SHARES A PASSION FOR BEADS

I have been allowed to be as crazy (excessive) as I want to be while creating this book. It has been an exceptional journey for me to allow my passions, my dreams and my actual life stories to become a manuscript. So awesome! Like I said in the my original confession there is a method to my madness, which is really gladness. I stopped along the way to have a good laugh. Now you know that "Stone Crazy" is a good description for part of my character. It's all about the bead! So I want to just confess a little more.

Remember my Dad's assembly line? That time is probably when I remember my first encounter with the beadbug up close and personal. My Dad was a real go getter. We were a family of eight so there was a lot of stuff going on in our household all of the time. Just getting ready for school each morning was an adventure. We had breakfast each morning and off to school we went. My siblings and I were the students the teacher could count on to show up every day, come rain, snow, sleet or hail. When we got home we did homework sitting around the table, knowing that in a short while our Dad would be home from work and we would eat dinner. Dinnertime was the best time of the day. We could eat and talk about the day's events. We could share conversations with our parents who really did sit at either end of the table. We often compared ourselves to the hit TV show The Brady Brunch. We even had a Marsha and great grandmother Vera was our Alice for a while. Now our mother was the primary caretaker and the chief disciplinarian. My father worked and gave orders as needed. My mother often yelled and yelled, while my father could command silence just by clearing his throat. He was a man of few words yet often when he spoke, what he said made us wonder. He told a lot of jokes too. Sometimes we were not sure if he was serious or joking. For instance, my father used to say: "whatever you choose to do, do it to death". I am certain now that he meant that whatever we chose to do in life, be the best or strive to complete each task as if your life depended on it. All six of his children are known to be very competitive. We do not consider second place a true victory. If you attended one of our game nights you would have an idea of what I'm talking about.

Game nights with Daddy were the best, especially when we played Monopoly. He would be the banker during the game and the rest of us were the players. As we became older the game became more intense. Yes, intensed because we used two boards instead of one to spice up the game and we dissolved all relationships during the time we played. Even spectators had fun watching us play while craving to be a part of the next session. Some of those sessions lasted for hours and there had to be a winner. I realize now there was another important lesson to consider in his words that I previously mentioned. Be a winner by finishing what you start.

Each day throughout the year 2009 I became closer to my golden days. My life was good but there seemed to be something missing. On New Year's Eve in the past I have found myself in numerous places other than the place we had to be as children: somebody's Church. The idea of praying my old year *out* and a new one *in*, actually seemed quite refreshing. Therefore, off to Church I went and something mystical happened! The Pastor of this Church: Bishop Maureen L. Davis gave a message this early morning titled: **"Victory is Mine in 2009-I Win"**. Everyone loves to be a winner. There is an unexplainable thrill that follows victory. Victorious is one way to describe my feelings that morning. I confess leaving that service with my mind, heart and soul on fire. I wanted the new life she talked about with God in it. Imagine a new life beginning with the first day of a new year by simply allowing the spirit of the Creator of Heaven and Earth into my life. This was one of the most powerful messages I have ever heard.

Now twenty days into the year I am about to witness history in the making. At the request of a neighbor I went to an Inaugural brunch, where I witnessed the induction of the 44th President of the United States: The Honorable Barrack H. Obama. He is a man of color who accomplished a major victory. As I watched the large monitor tears begin to flow from my eyes and down my face. They were happy tears. They were proud tears. As my new First Family appeared, my heart began to beat in a different rhythm. At that moment I said to myself "if this man can achieve this status in my lifetime, I want to do something extraordinary and victorious too. I want to write a book! Write a book? Ok, although I had no idea what the contents would be: I thought about my brother Nate who happens to be the Author of a book titled "A Different Breed of Brother" published in the year 2000. He was the first in our family to accomplish such a task. During that time, the thought of writing something of my own never crossed my mind. I shared my idea with the person sitting next to me. He became very excited for me. He suggested that I get started right away. Before leaving he took a picture with me then gave me a business card. To my surprise I shared my dream with a Federal Court Judge. No wonder Beadsz had to face a Judge, lol. I experienced another teary-eyed moment as I reminisced our conversation during the ceremony. My dream of writing and publishing a story became inevitable.

I began to explore my passions. Then one morning I woke up with a poem on my mind about beads. I am sure I went to sleep the previous night with a bead magazine. Let me tell you that when you are passionate about something you can write about it, talk about it and even sing about it. Everyone has a passion. You just have to discover what it is. Once discovered, the sky is the limit! Who would have guessed that a book confessing a bead passion could evolve without trying to teach anyone the actual the craft of beading.

ACCOMPLISHING ANYTHING REQUIRES THAT YOU FINISH WHAT YOU START, REVISING THE WORDS OF MY FATHER. COMPLETION IS HOW BEADED DESIGNS BECOME WONDERFUL CREATIONS. IF YOU WANT TO DISCOVER YOUR PASSIONATE SIDE, I ENCOURAGE YOU TO ACCEPT THE CHALLENGE TO B.E.A.D.

B.E.A.D.

BECOME EXCITED ABOUT DREAMING

About what you want to accomplish

B.E.A.D.

BECOME EXCITED ABOUT DOING

What ever it takes to fulfill your dreams.

B.E.A.D.

BECOME EXCITED ABOUT DESTINY

The place where dreams can take you!

B.E.A.D.!   B.E.A.D.!   B.E.A.D.!

THE B.E.(A.D.) GINNING

ONE WHO SEES BEADS IN A NEW LIGHT

You have reached the last chapter of this book yet the beginning of my renewed passion for beads. I will be making my most precious confessions right here-right now. While searching for definitions for the word bead to help me understand my bead passion, Webster described a bead as: a small material pierced for stringing. When I looked up the word bead in the Old English Dictionary; the definition states that "bead" comes from the greek word bebe; which also means prayer. I confess that I became stone crazy about beads all over again. I see beads in a new light . My designs reflect this light too by using more precious stones and crystal (stones that bling). Make sure your seatbelt is still secure; we are going deep before coming in!

In the previous chapter I discussed the end of my first bead adventure as it pertains to dreaming naturally. Now I want to take you on an adventure that requires dreaming supernaturally using prayer, communicating with God.

A prayer can be a B.E.A.D. or Best Extraordinary Anytime Destination that a person can reach without leaving the earth. Talk about an amazing ride! You see prayer gives you the ability to not only dream but the ability to find creative ways to turn the most impossible dreams into reality. I found out that prayer has superpower. It is a *stone* that has the ability to defeat any *Goliath* that life places into your path to success. So I now confess that I am a beader who is also a believer in the power of prayer. My prayer (bead) confession of belief was made on that wonderful New Year's Day January 1, 2009.

I accepted the *materials* (God's Word) needed to *string* (put together) everything this new life has to offer. God's Word, also known as The Holy Scriptures or The Bible is the *Believer's Creed* full of *seed beads, precious stones*, and *hidden treasures* too.

From the time I made my spiritual confession to believe (John 3:16), I became a B.E.A.D. (prayer) B.U.G., Blessed Exceedingly Above Dreams * Blessed Under Grace, a new person (2Corinthians 5:17). I don't even think the same way I did before 2009 and my new creative thoughts continually (Romans 12:2) amaze me. Remember when I began my story: I described the word confession as a spring cleaning and a fall organizing of the mind. A prayer of confesion that I am a sinner saved by grace gave my mind, heart, and soul a spiritual cleansing that is breathtakingly beautiful and full of bling. The more I read the Holy Scriptures, the more **bling** I feel in my being! The Bible is unique and one of a kind. It is like no other book. The prayers found in it alone are priceless. The Lord's Prayer (Matthew 6:9) can get any dream ready for lift off. Then the prayer in Psalms 23 will get you off the ground. The prayer in Psalms 27 lets me know where to find light and direction while going down the path of life. Now if you want to boldly go where you have never gone before; I challenge you to read the Scriptures and pray too. This combination is superfuel for any destination that seems impossible (Philippians 4:13).

Beadaholique (bead-a-holic) is a word I encountered while reading a bead magazine. Holics are usually the movers and shakers of whatever they choose to do because they do it excessively and sometimes to death (ironically). An alcoholic drinks excessively. A shopaholic shops excessively. A gambler who excessively plays games of chance is also considered a holic. These excessive behaviors often leave you with an unhealthy addiction. Beadaholiques are the opposite. We represent a healthy addiction. This is true naturally and spiritually. They love to bead and bead (pray). They live to bead and bead (pray). They can bead (pray) all day and all night which sounds excessive but in a positive way! The more they practice beading (praying) the more stone like they become. A Stone (solid) Crazy (excessive) Beadaholique (Pray-er) is someone who can achieve impossible dreams.

Sharing both of my bead worlds has been truly adventurous, especially the times when I was beading and got stuck in life (craftmania). The bead patrol agents (angels) had to be called. They came to my rescue, arrested me with beaded bangles (Ephesians 6:14-15) and carried me off to Beadville; a secret place (Psalms 91). A place where you can get what you need from a bead (prayer). It is a place where transformations take place. Supernatural transformation! When natural meets super you get creativeness to the highest power or beadaliousity all over again! I confess being stuck in craftmania many times in 2009. The entire year was full of challenges. It was the gospel treasures (God's word) and prayers (beads) strung through my mind, heart and soul that carried me through to victory. Victory feels good. Victory looks good. Victory shows up and shows out just like bling does on things that I see in my dreams. Victory is truly rewarding!

I mentioned earlier, Man was formed from the dust of the earth (Genesis 2:7). Precious gemstones are found within the dust of the earth. Precious gemstones are mentioned throughout God's Word. If I were to name every *kind* of precious stone found in the earth not one could compare to *mankind*. Each one of us was created to be truly unique from the other. Just like the beautiful stones that are discovered in the earth a natural beauty exists in everyone. Then some gems find themselves placed into the hands of a Sculptor, who takes them through a process that will make them extraordinarily beautiful. Likewise God's Human Gems also go through a process that allow us to become true beauties, never plain, but extraordinary if we accept God's path for our lives.

Accept God's bead path by: Becoming Extraordinary After Deliverance (2 Corinthians 5:17) a new person! A BEADaholique that is Stone Crazy about the Word of God. The word that can transform an already *Beautiful Unique Gemstone into a precious, priceless and powerful one that out sparkles* the rest. **Life does not mean anything if it does not have bling!** Make a difference in this world by accepting God's stringing medians: love, hope, peace and joy. Sharing and showing Love everywhere you go. God's Love (Psalm 63:3) is expressed in ways yet to be discovered. I've found this love in a smile, a song, a poem, a book, clothing designs, art designs, jewelry designs and more. Just know that God has promised that with him whatever you do pray(bead) first, and you will receive direction (Proverbs 3:6). A Spiritual Beaded Path; Imagine that!

Before the year 2010 ends, I will officially be a Golden Girl with a red white and gray card (AARP) to prove it. LOL. I know the future holds more beading adventures, but I confess that I am now experiencing Heaven on Earth and I am bound for Heaven Above. Heaven above has streets of gold and buildings made with walls of precious stones (Revelations 21:21) so I can be Stone Crazy in this life and Stone Crazy in my life to come. I leave you with my final confession: I have:

BECOME EXCITED ABOUT DESTINATION SUCCESS Z (to infinity and beyond) BEADSZ. WITHOUT WORRY I CAN JUST **BEAD HAPPY, allowing God's Love to Show Me The Way.**

God's Love Shows Me The Way
(the new beadbug song)

Chorus: *God's love shows me the way God's love shows me the way*

Each and every day yeah God's love shows me the way

God's love shows me the way God's love shows me the way

Each and every day yeah God's love shows me the way

Verse: There are some days when life gets in the way

 I can't talk I can't walk I can't fight

Whatever I choose to do I have to make it through

So I pray with all of my might

Chorus: *God's love shows me the way God's love shows me the way*

Each and every day yeah God's love shows me the way

God's love shows me the way God's love shows me the way

Each and every day yeah God's love shows me the way

End: *God's love shows me the way.............ay*

FREEDOM

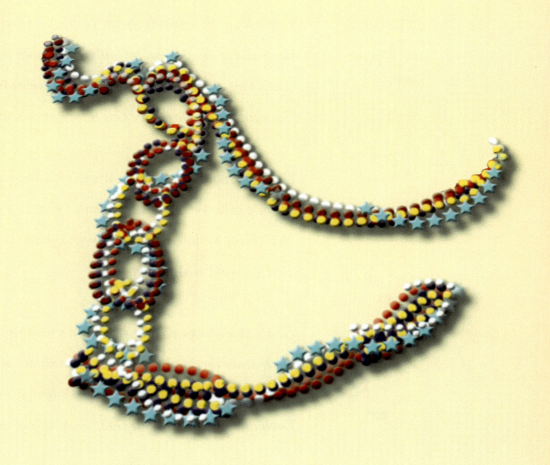

Printed in the United States
By Bookmasters